Contents

P9-DNL-209

Introduction

This volume is designed for all guitarists. Arranged for quick, easy reference, it contains 101 stylistic phrases, commonly known as "licks"—those essential, self-contained instrumental figures utilized by the great masters. Licks are part and parcel of the jazz tradition and the jazz experience. Charlie Parker used 'em, so did John Coltrane and Wes Montgomery, and so does virtually every player on the current scene. Licks are short, meaningful passages skillfully tucked into tunes and riffs, and laced through the improvised solos of the repertory. The audience may not hear them or even be aware of them, but they can always be felt. A well-turned lick can make the difference between a cold, mechanical statement and a communicative, engaging performance; and the right lick driven by the energy and conviction of a seasoned player can bring the audience to its feet.

Now you can add an authentic jazz feel and flavor to your playing. Here are 101 definitive licks from every major jazz guitar style neatly organized into easy-to-use categories. They're all here: swing jazz, pre-bop, bebop, hard bop, modal jazz, cool jazz, soul jazz, postmodern jazz, free jazz, chord licks, and more. Browse to your heart's content, and feel free to tap into the feeling of each lick that speaks to you. As you do, you'll be taking that vital first step of reinvention that connects you to the spirit and the essence of America's most emotional and transcendent art music.

Tips for Using this Book and CD

1. Play these licks all over the fingerboard. If a lick is positioned at the eighth fret, move it down to the third fret and play it in that area; you will notice that the string feel, tension, and fret distances have a bearing on how the lick feels. Then move it up chromatically as a drill, playing it in every position from the third to the seventeenth fret. This will depend on the range of your guitar's fingerboard. Note the key changes as you move the licks to different positions.

2. Put several licks into the same key. For example, if a lick is presented in C and another is in G, place them both into C, and then into G. This is the musical equivalent of using all your linguistic phrases in one conversation.

3. Take that collection of phrases into various keys. Once you have grouped a number of licks into the same key, move that grouping to new positions.

4. Make notes, mental or written, about the feel of each lick. Your visceral, emotional reaction to a lick is part of the ad-lib selection process when improvising. This process could involve forming a visual image of the lick's physical shape—how it sits on the fingerboard.

5. Add at least one new lick per week to your vocabulary. Memorize and *use it* in your current musical situation—playing with a band, adding it to an existing solo or song, or when jamming with your friends.

About the Recording

Each lick is played twice on the accompanying audio: first at the normal tempo and then, after a two-and-a-half-second pause, at a slower tempo.

Licks 1-98 are found at the corresponding CD counter numbers. Licks 99, 100, and 101 are presented as a single track on number 99. Within that counter number (99), use the following time codes to find the three licks: Lick 99 occurs at 0:00, Lick 100 occurs at 0:45, and Lick 101 at 1:04.

These licks were played using authentic Gibson archtop electric guitars and miked amplifiers including vintage Gibson and Fender tube amps and modern Polytone amps. The sounds, settings, and particular instruments are cited in the accompanying performance notes.

Lick Analysis and the Lick Legend

Licks are the musical sentences of the jazz language. Part of learning, understanding, and mastering a language involves studying the "basic parts of speech." The following terms and their abbreviations are used to define these specific elements at work in the licks—they are used to diagram the jazz sentences, so to speak. The abbreviations are used throughout in lieu of text blurbs to provide a streamlined but thorough approach to lick analysis.

The Lick Legend

Single melody tones are cited and circled in the music notation. These include:

LT=Leading tone. A leading tone pushes toward an important melodic tone from a half step below—in jazz, typically to the root, 3rd, 5th, or 7th or to a nonharmonic tone.

LN=Lower neighbor. A note either a half step or whole step below a principal tone. A lower neighbor is typically preceded and followed ("sandwiched") by the note that it decorates.

NH=Nonharmonic tone. These would include the 2nd or 9th, 4th or 11th, 6th or 13th, and major 7th degrees of the scale.

BN=Blue note. These include the flatted 5th/augmented 4th, the minor 3rd in a major or dominant context, and the minor 7th.

ACT=Altered chord tone(s). These would include the flatted 5th and 9th, and augmented 5th and 9th.

Larger structural devices such as specific figures of three notes or greater, noteworthy scales, theme or song quotes, and turnarounds are cited and bracketed in the notation. These include:

ARP=Arpeggio. At least three notes preceded by a corresponding chord name, such as "C arp."

CA=Chromatic ascent. Three or more chromatic notes in a row moving higher in pitch.

CD=Chromatic descent. Three or more chromatic notes in a row moving lower in pitch. In jazz, chromatic descents can be "decorated" as in Licks 2, 12, 17, 52, 58, 64, and 67.

RM=Reverse mordent. A three-note ornament commonly found in jazz. It involves the alternation of a main note with its upper neighbor.

PED=Pedal tone(s). These are repeated notes within a musical passage. In jazz, these are often alternated with a primary stepwise or chromatic melody.

RF=Repeated figure. These are the basis for the riff concept of jazz and blues.

IMIT=Imitative procedure at work.

SEQ=Sequence. An imitative procedure involving the repetition of a figure on different scale steps.

TF=Target figure. This three-note melody pattern typically approaches a selected (target) tone by beginning on its upper neighbor, jumping to its lower neighbor, and then moving to the target. See Lick 20.

VLF=Voice leading figure. A specific four-note pattern endemic to bebop and modern jazz styles. The all-important figure involves approaching a particular note first from a half step above and then from below (always by two half steps in succession). See Lick 20.

SUB=Substitution. This refers to an alternate scale or melody substituted for a primary relationship. It is followed by a scale or chord name, such as "SUB A♭m" (A♭ minor instead of a more typical B♭7 scale or harmony). See Lick 27.

Q: and A:=Question and answer phrases. The "call-and-response" procedure is an important aspect of applying licks to form a larger melody structure.

Every lick is defined by an overall context; this can be a "basic scale" or "basic tonality." Most jazz licks are defined by their harmonic setting and use a variety of scales to convey melodic motion through chord changes. In this case, a single basic scale would not be a sufficient label and could present an incomplete and erroneous picture. Melodies such as these are labeled as having a "basic tonality" though they are comprised of single notes as in Lick 10. Many jazz licks have a plural harmonic application. For example, Lick 1 can be thought of as originating from either the A♭ major scale or the A♭ Mixolydian mode (dominant seventh sound) as it does not contain the crucial seventh in its melody. Similarly, Lick 5 has a plural application and could be used over an Fm6 or B♭9 chord background.

A suggested tempo is provided for each lick—Fast Swing, Moderately, Slowly (Rubato), etc.—to further guide you in applying these phrases in your music. All licks marked with a swing feel (Fast Swing, Moderate Swing, etc.) are to be perceived as occuring against a triplet feel background and are generally to be played with swing eighth-note rhythm. This means that each two-eighth-note rhythm unit is to be played as a quarter-eighth grouping of an eighth-note triplet (♫ = ♩♪).

After getting these licks under your fingers, try taking them apart by playing them in pieces, inside out and backwards. Each lick can be thought of as having several melodic or harmonic "cells" of varied sizes in its structure. Each cell is akin to a thought or group of words in a sentence. These can be grafted to other cells from other licks to form new phrases. This process of developing original music from fragments is a viable strategy for building a new musical statements of your own.

Finally, once you have grasped the essentials of these licks, begin your own investigations. To this end, a list of suggested recordings is offered in the back pages of this volume. Pick your favorite jazz improvisations, and listen for these devices at work in the music of the great players. Be on the lookout for imitative procedures and sequential activity in melodies and riffs, question-and-answer phrases, harmonic extensions and alterations, unique turnarounds, and other thematic development strategies. This sort of listening and thinking opens the door to a deeper understanding and assimilation of the jazz language.

Swing and Pre-Bop

The first group of licks comes from the swing era of the late 1930s and early 1940s. Jazz was at the height of its popularity in this period. Swing was a dance-oriented jazz style played predominately in ballrooms by big bands of fourteen or more musicians. The music's harmony centered around mildly dissonant chords like major and minor triads with added sixths, dominant sevenths, and dominant ninths. These harmonies supported largely diatonic melodies set in riff-dominated jazz tunes, 12-bar blues structures, and 32-bar pop tunes.

Swing's leading guitarist was Charlie Christian, who combined elements of earlier classic jazz traditions as well as blues licks from the southern states and horn licks borrowed from wind players like Lester Young and Roy Eldridge. The practice of emulating and adapting "horn licks" (largely from saxophone and trumpet) has been a mainstay of jazz guitar since Christian's time. Christian's pioneering use of the newly-designed Gibson Electric-Spanish (ES) guitar established the role of the electric guitarist in jazz. Prior to his appearance, jazz guitarists were mainly confined to strumming in the rhythm section or forced to play in smaller all-string combos such as Django Reinhardt's Hot Club quintet.

Christian's work with the Benny Goodman Sextet set the standard for early combos that included electric guitar. Jazz, blues, and pop guitarists who followed in the 1940s were under the spell of Charlie Christian and sought to emulate his sound and style. In swing and pre-bop, this included Oscar Moore, Barney Kessel, Al Casey, Herb Ellis, and others. Sweepingly influential, Christian's licks were also heard in the subsequent wave of jump blues guitarists and early rock 'n' roll players. Identifiers of the swing style include an eighth-note-dominated horn-like phrasing, extensive use of the sixth degree of the scale and chromatic passing tones, blues riffs, and a strong swing rhythm feel.

To maintain sonic authenticity, I played these licks on my Gibson ES-175/CC with heavy-gauge strings. This instrument is equipped with the early Gibson bar pickup (dubbed the "Charlie Christian pickup") in the neck position. The volume and tone controls were both set at 8. The guitar was played through a vintage 1952 Gibson GA-75 amp with one 15-inch speaker. The tone of the amp was set for a warm and moderately clean sound with a hint of tube overdrive; in this case, treble and bass at the midway point and the volume at just below halfway. This sound is generally the norm for early jazz guitar, circa 1940s-1950s.

1 **Basic Scale: A♭ Major/Mixolydian**

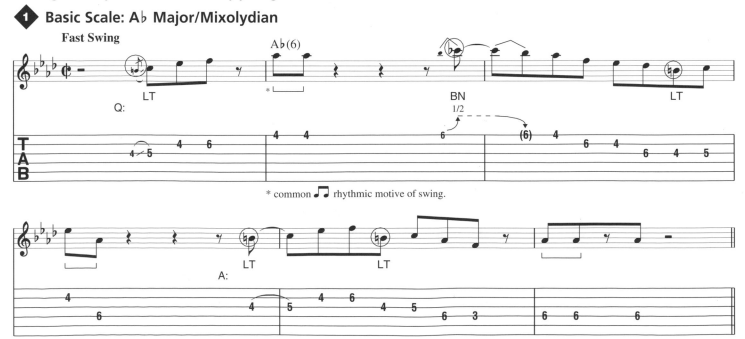

*common ♪♪ rhythmic motive of swing.

2 ▸ Basic Scale: C Mixolydian

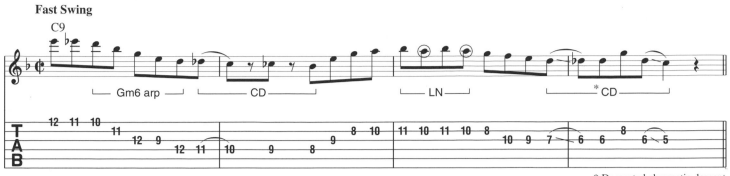

Fast Swing

*Decorated chromatic descent.

3 ▸ Basic Scale: G Mixolydian

Fast Swing

4 ▸ Basic Scale: G Blues

Moderately Fast Swing

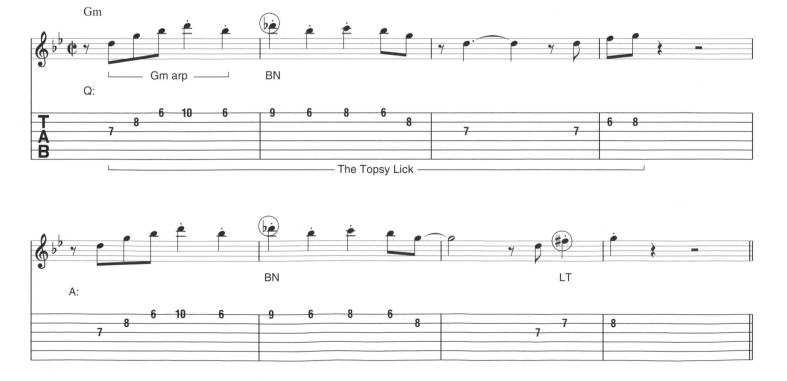

The Topsy Lick

5 Basic Tonality: Fm6/B♭9

6 Basic Scale: C Major

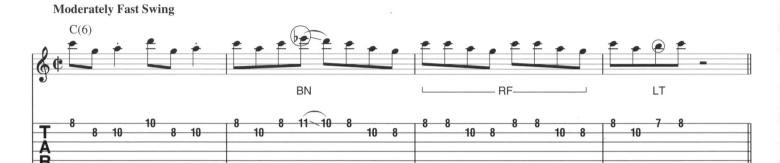

7 Basic Scale: C Mixolydian

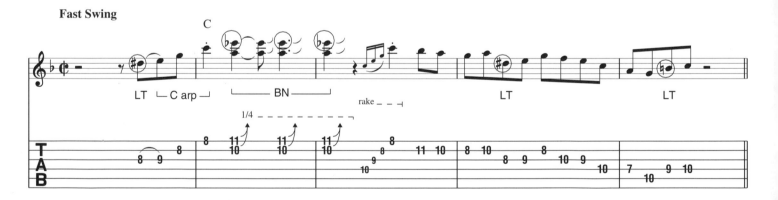

8 Basic Tonality: A Dominant—D Dominant

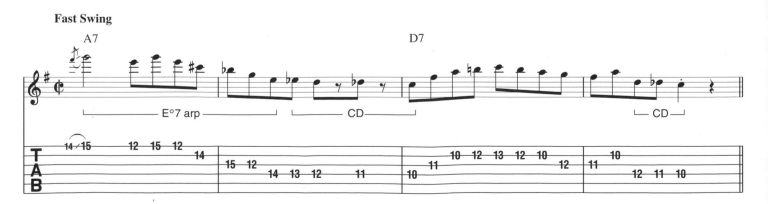

9 Basic Tonality: F Major/F Mixolydian

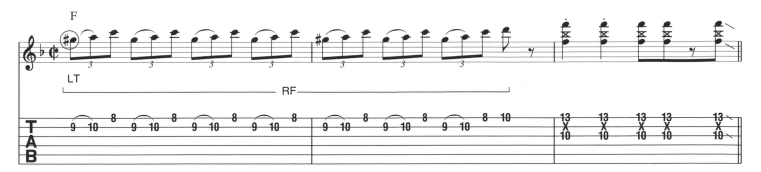

10 Basic Tonality: C Major

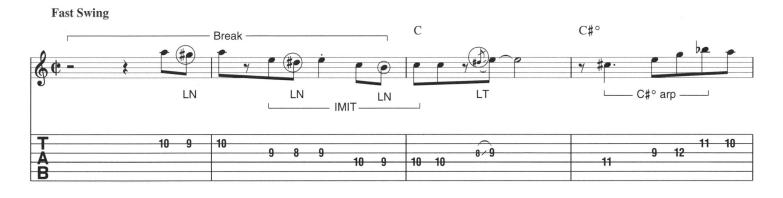

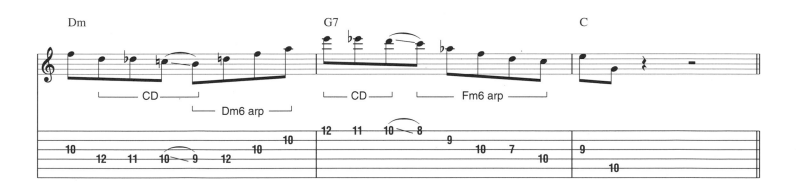

11 Basic Scale: F Mixolydian

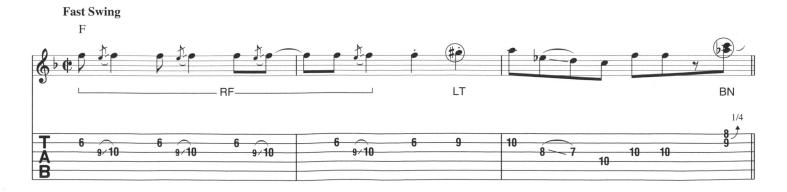

12 Basic Scale: G Mixolydian

Fast Swing

13 Basic Tonality: F Dominant

Moderately Fast *

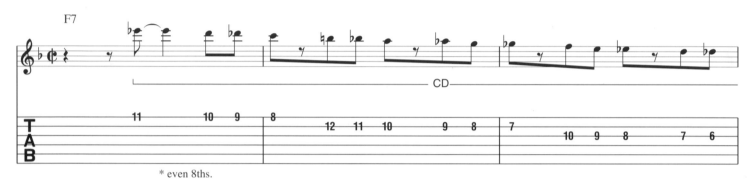

* even 8ths.

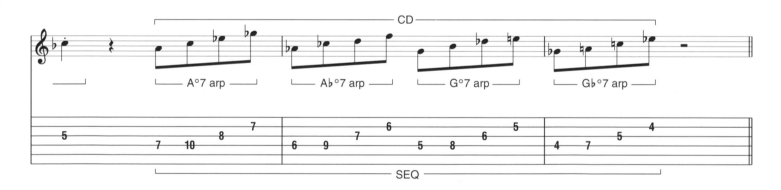

14 Basic Scale: B♭ Dorian

Fast Swing

Bebop
Bird: Charlie Parker

Bebop evolved as the primary dialect of jazz following the swing era of the 1940s. This branch of the jazz language, built on the foundation of the earlier swing style, increased dissonance levels, introduced more chromaticism, used altered chords and harmonic substitutions freely, and generally stretched the musical envelope of the art form. Alto saxophonist Charlie Parker was the leading voice of bebop and had a tremendous impact on the entire art of jazz after his arrival in the 1940s. His licks became the lingua franca of modern jazz. Transferring and translating horn licks (and those from other instruments) to the guitar is an important aspect of developing a jazz vocabulary since much of the basic language of jazz was first established by wind and keyboard players. Such is the thrust of this section, which presents some of Bird's favorite sax licks adapted here for guitar. Throughout this batch of licks, you will notice many variations on the pattern labeled VLF (*Voice leading figure*—see The Lick Legend on pp. 6-7). This melodic encircling figure was popularized by Charlie Parker in his improvising and composing, and is a definitive device used to approach significant chord tones in a passage. It probably originated from Duke Ellington's 1940 "Concerto for Cootie." Another favorite bebop device (again involving the application of borrowed materials) was the use of song quotes in improvisation. Popular song quotes favored by Parker and tucked into solos include "Honeysuckle Rose" (The Honey Lick), "A Table in the Corner" (The Table Lick), and "I Thought About You" (Thought About You Lick).

These licks were played on my new Gibson ES-175D with heavy-gauge flatwound strings plugged into a Polytone Mini-Brute II amp with a 12-inch speaker. The guitar's neck pickup was used exclusively with the volume rolled down to about 7 or 8 and the tone at 8. The amp was set to attenuate highs and bass (there's plenty with an archtop guitar) and enhance the midrange, and to add some spring reverb. This sound is generally depictive of today's standard bop guitar tone.

15 **Basic Tonality: F Major/Dominant**

16 **Basic Tonality: A♭ Major—C Minor**

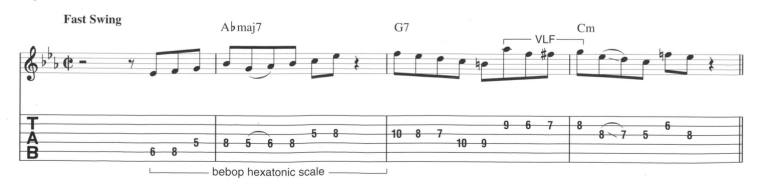

17 Basic Tonality: B♭ Major/Dominant

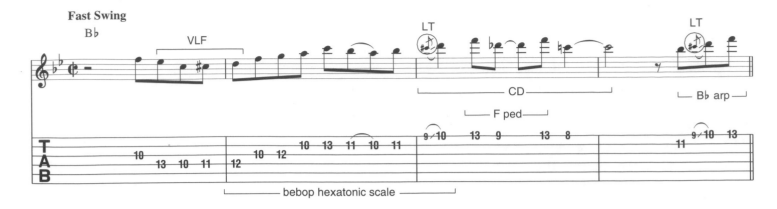

18 Basic Tonality: E♭ Dominant—B♭ Dominant

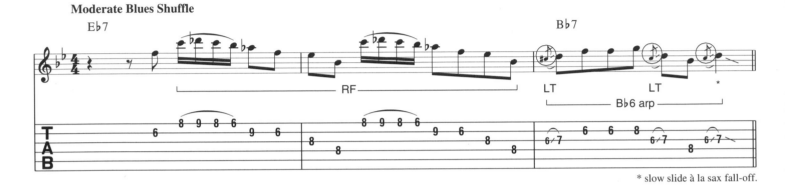

*slow slide à la sax fall-off.

19 Basic Tonality: G Major/Dominant

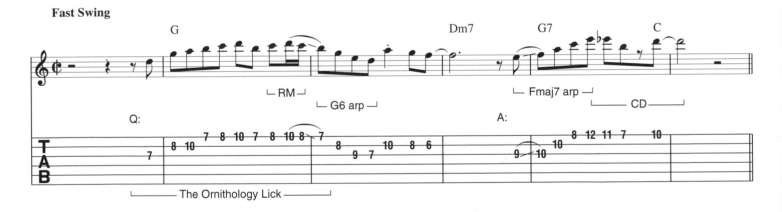

20 Basic Tonality: B♭ Major

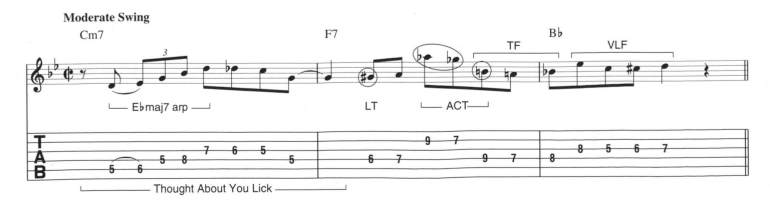

21 ▸ Basic Tonality: C Major

Moderately Fast Swing

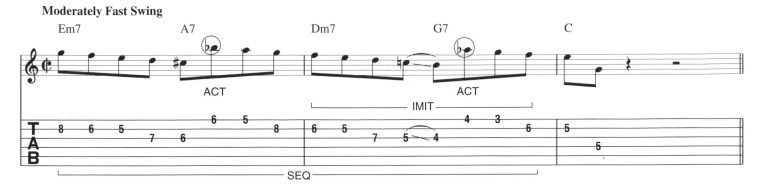

22 ▸ Basic Scale: B♭ Mixolydian/Blues

Moderate Swing

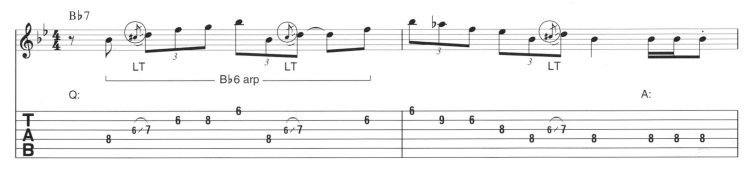

23 ▸ Basic Tonality: F Major

Fast Swing

24 Basic Tonality: G Major

Fast Swing

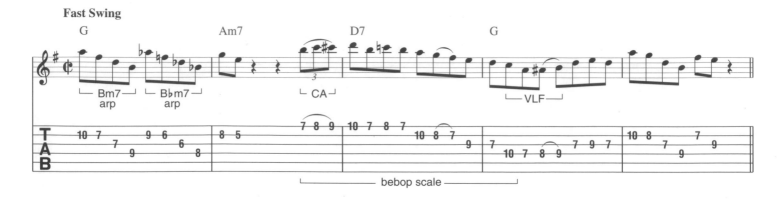

bebop scale

25 Basic Tonality: D Minor

Moderate Swing

26 Basic Tonality: B♭ Major

Fast Swing

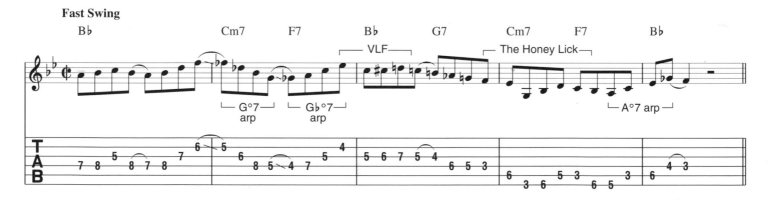

27 Basic Tonality: E♭ Major

Fast Swing

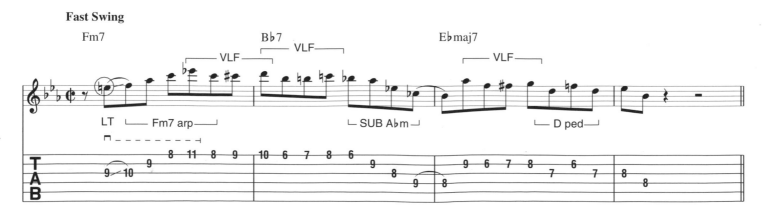

28 Basic Tonality: B♭ Major

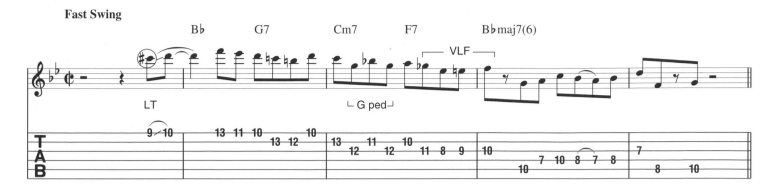

29 Basic Tonality: F Major

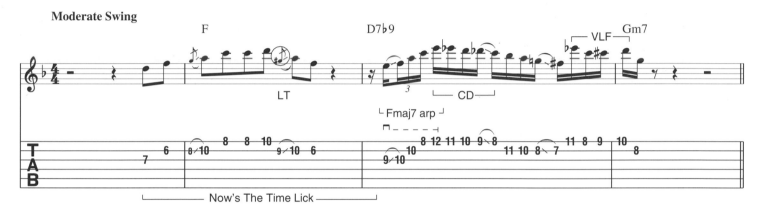

30 Basic Tonality: E♭ Major

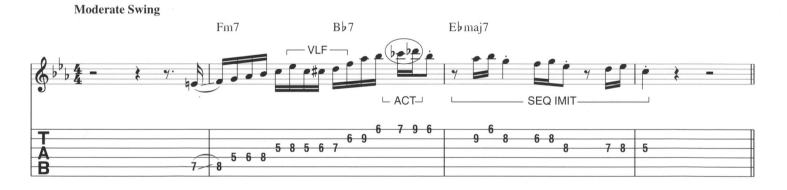

31 Basic Tonality: F Minor

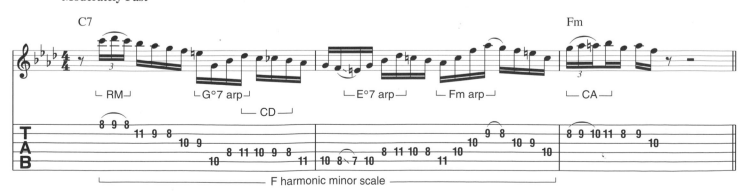

Post-Parker Bop Guitar

By the late 1940s, most post-Charlie Christian jazz guitarists were striving to incorporate horn-based bebop concepts and phraseology into their improvisations. Following the lead of wind players Charlie Parker, Dizzy Gillespie, Stan Getz, and Dexter Gordon, guitarists such as Barney Kessel, Tal Farlow, Jimmy Raney, Chuck Wayne, and Hank Garland personified the new movement. These innovations are reflected in the next set of licks. Notice the use of bebop components such as the Parker-inspired VLF motive, song quotes, horn-like phrasing, the bebop scale, extended and altered chord sounds, and the genre's greater overall dissonance. The melding of classic swing and jump blues melodies with bebop horn lines remains the basis for today's straight-ahead jazz guitar lexicon.

Guitarists of this period continued to favor Gibson archtop electrics fitted with a Charlie Christian bar pickup usually played through Gibson combo amps. Accordingly, these licks were played again with my Gibson ES-175/CC and Gibson GA-75 amp. Many jazz guitarists of yesteryear plugged into the microphone input (instead of the Instrument input) of their Gibson combos to employ the extra stage of preamplification. This is what you'll hear on these licks.

32 **Basic Tonality: D Minor**

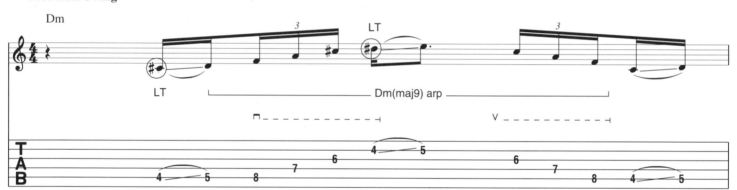

33 Basic Tonality: B♭ Major

Fast Swing

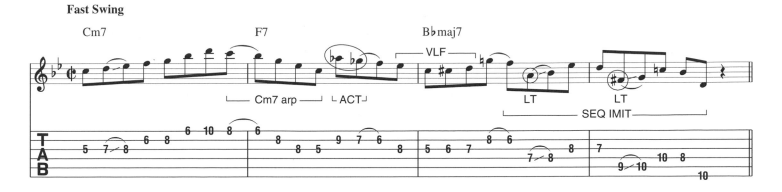

34 Basic Tonality: C Major

Moderate Swing

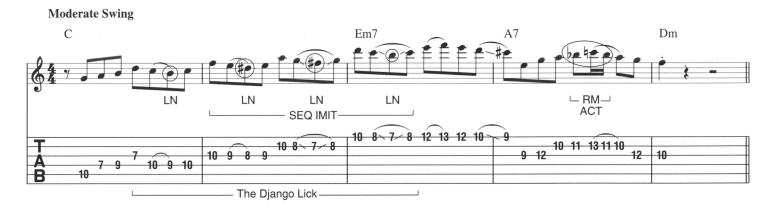

35 Basic Tonality: Cycle of Fourths progression

Fast Swing

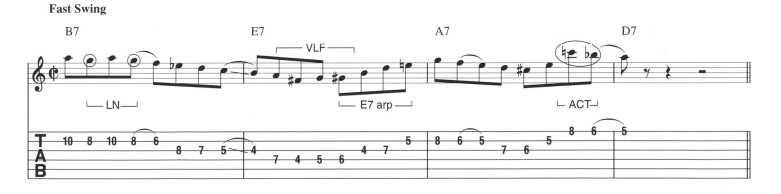

36 Basic Tonality: B♭ Major

Moderately Fast Swing

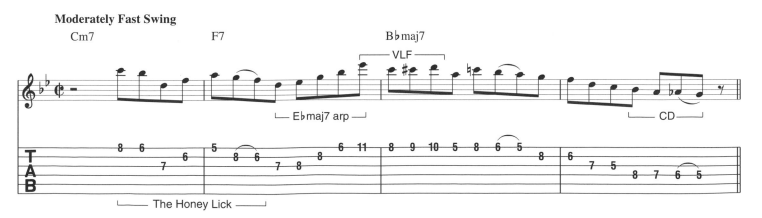

37 Basic Tonality: B♭ Major

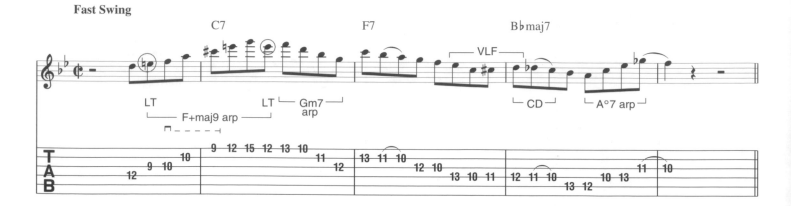

38 Basic Tonality: F Major

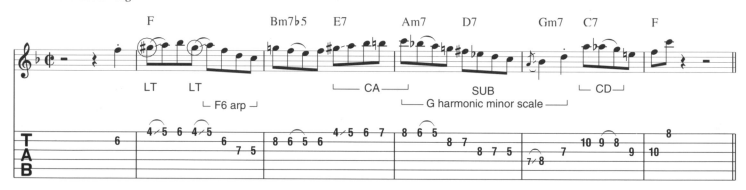

39 Basic Tonality: D Minor

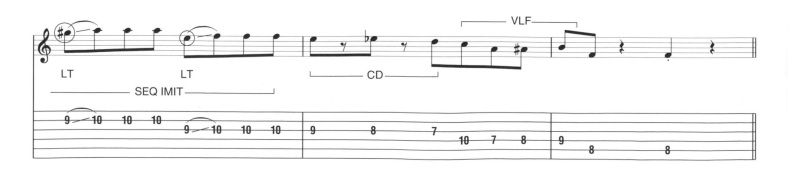

Post-Bop Modern Jazz
Trane: John Coltrane

Tenor saxophonist John Coltrane was as pivotal to the next phase of jazz (post-bop) as Charlie Parker was to bebop. He was the leading voice of the style and its prime innovator in the late 1950s and early 1960s. Like Parker, many of Trane's innovations became standard operating procedures in jazz—utilized by all its instrumentalists including guitarists. With Trane, *double-timing* (playing phrases dominated by sixteenth notes rather than by eighth notes) became a standard device in jazz. Further aspects of his contributions to the post-bop jazz vernacular include more florid bebop-oriented playing and adventurous harmonic substitutions—which when combined received the label "sheets of sound." Trane also increased levels of dissonance and used more distant extended chord relationships than had been found in bebop. Like many bebop players, Coltrane utilized fragments of pop songs in his improvising. His favorite quotes are now standard pieces in the vocabulary of jazz. They include "All This and Heaven Too" (The Heaven Lick), "While My Lady Sleeps" (While My Lady Sleeps Lick), and "Pop Goes the Weasel" (The Weasel Lick). Trane also explored exotic scales in his playing. His signature use of the *symmetrical diminished scale* (alternating half step-whole step scale) is found in Lick 49. In retrospect, Trane bridged the gap from bebop to the hard bop and modal styles to come and anticipated the free jazz style of the 1960s.

I played these licks with a new Gibson ES-175D and a Polytone Mini-Brute II amp.

40 **Basic Tonality: C Major**

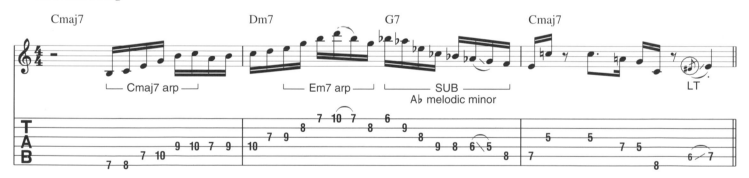

41 **Basic Tonality: G Major**

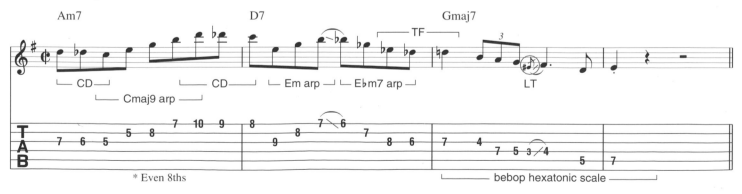

42 Basic Tonality: C Major

Moderate Swing

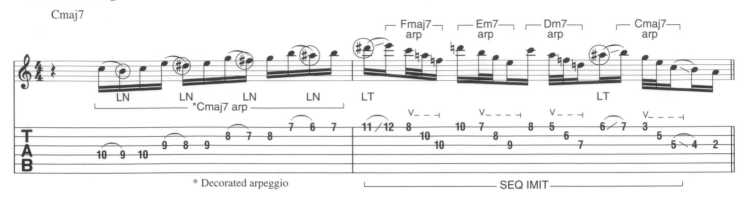

* Decorated arpeggio

43 Basic Tonality: B♭ Major

Moderately Fast Swing

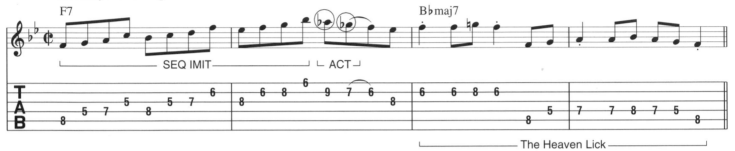

44 Basic Tonality: D Minor

Fast Swing

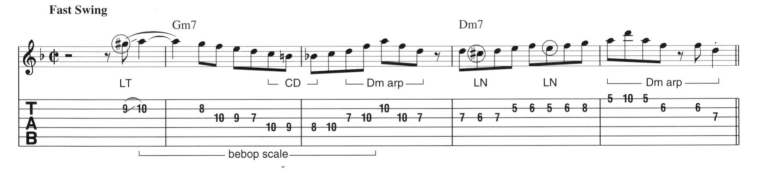

45 Basic Tonality: C Minor

Fast Swing

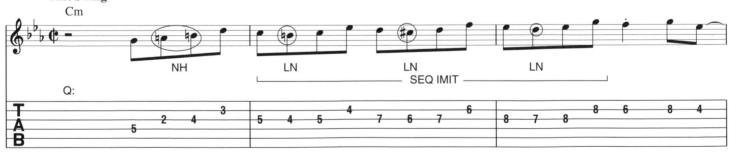

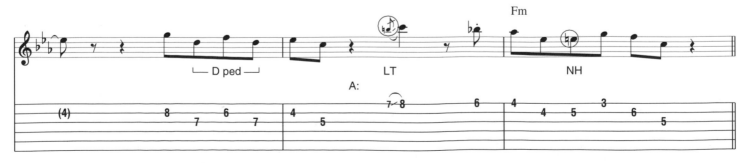

46 Basic Tonality: C Major

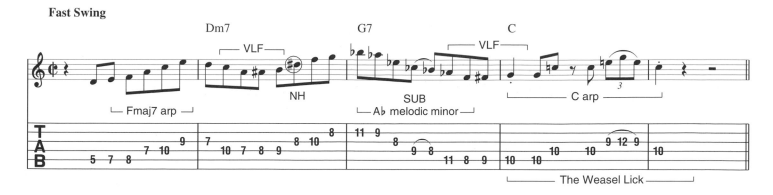

47 Basic Tonality: G Dominant

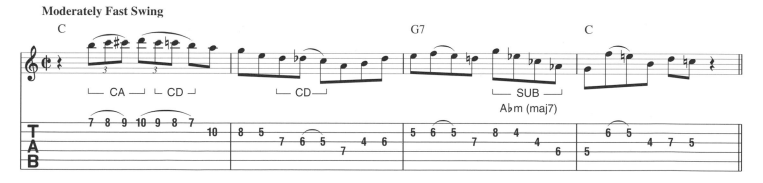

48 Basic Tonality: C Major

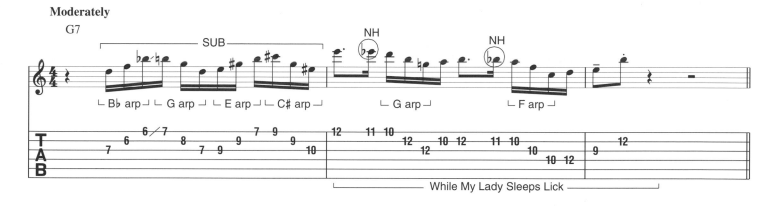

49 Basic Scale: E Diminished

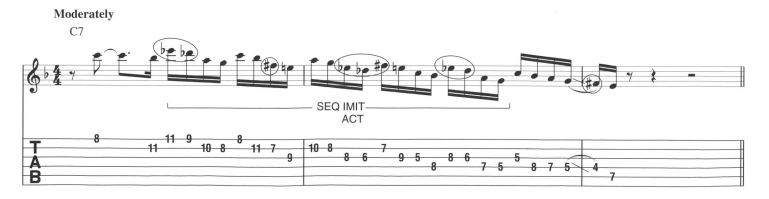

Hard Bop and Cool Jazz

Hard bop and cool jazz started out as subsidiary branches of bop. Both grew as a response to the growing complexities of bebop. Hard bop evolved in the early 1950s and is distinguished by equally fast burning bebop tempos, but with simpler melodies, a pronounced rhythm 'n' blues and funk influence and catchier rhythms. Cool jazz (sometimes called "West Coast jazz") appeared somewhat earlier: Most cite Miles Davis's auspicious 1950 record *Birth of the Cool* as a definitive starting point. Like hard bop, cool jazz was characterized as a simplification of the earlier bebop style, but favored slower tempos and a quieter, more relaxed execution and, perhaps, a more cerebral approach to improvising. Both hard bop and cool jazz were influential throughout the 1950s. Guitarists associated with cool jazz include Jim Hall, Billy Bauer, and Johnny Smith. Wes Montgomery is universally acknowledged as the quintessential hard bop guitarist. Other significant hard bop players are Grant Green, Kenny Burrell, Howard Roberts, and Joe Pass.

I played these licks with a 1956 Gibson ES-175D with P-90 pickups. The guitar was strung with medium-heavy gauge strings and the neck pickup was used exclusively. The amplifier was one of the great all-time jazz combos, a Fender '65 Twin-Reverb with two 12-inch speakers. The bright switch was not engaged, and the tone controls were set to produce a warm but clean sound with an emphasis on the midrange.

50 Basic Tonality: C Major

Moderate Swing

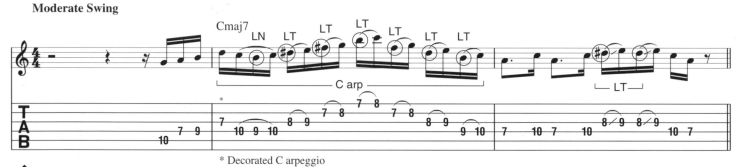

* Decorated C arpeggio

51 Basic Tonality: C Major

Moderately Fast Swing

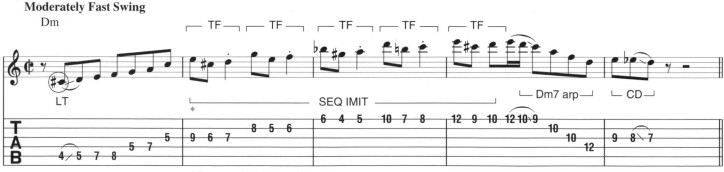

* Decorated Em7 arpeggio

52 Basic Tonality: B Minor

Moderately

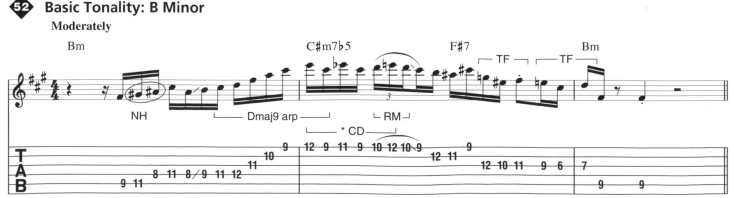

* Decorated chromatic descent

53 Basic Tonality: B♭ Major

Moderate Jazz Waltz (with Swing Feel)

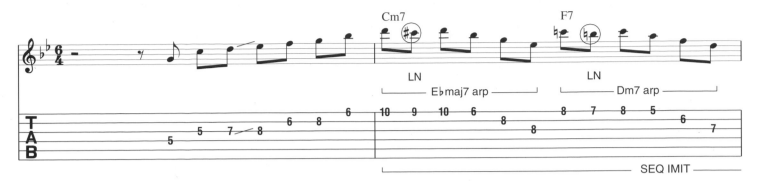

54 Basic Tonality: G Major Blues

Moderate Swing

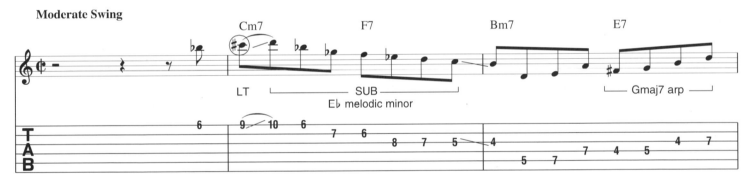

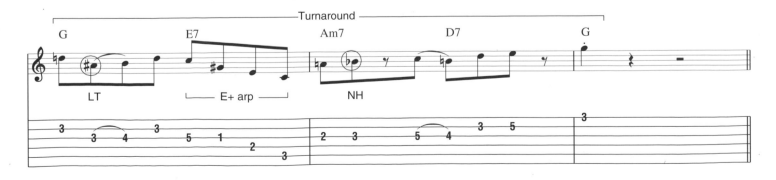

55 Basic Tonality: F Dominant

Moderate Swing

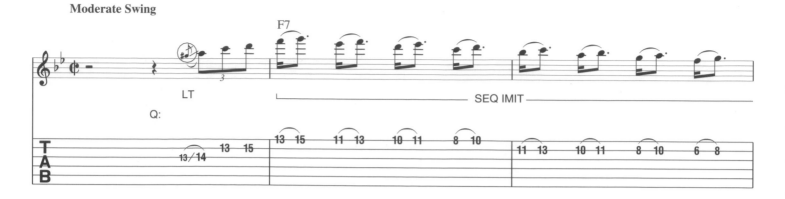

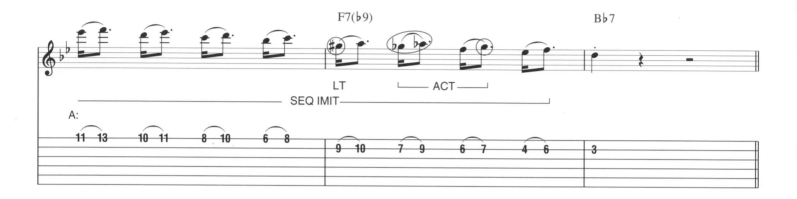

56 Basic Tonality: E Minor

Moderately Fast Swing

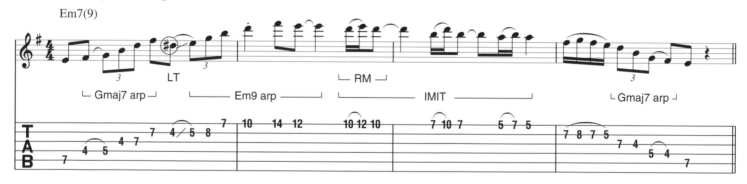

57 Basic Tonality: G Major

Moderately

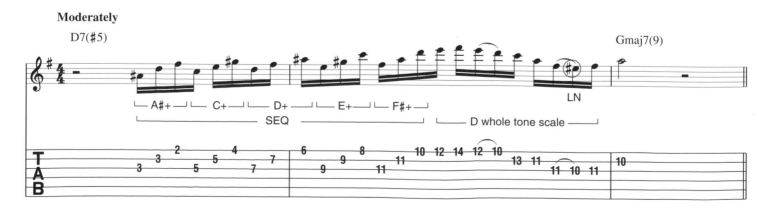

58 Basic Tonality: C Minor

Moderate Latin Jazz

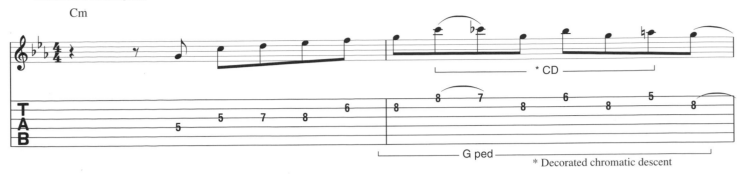

* Decorated chromatic descent

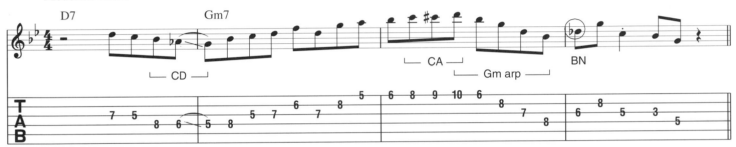

59 Basic Tonality: G Minor

Moderate Latin

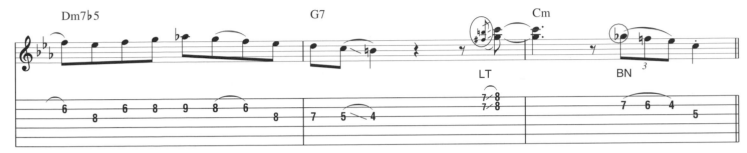

60 Basic Tonality: G Major

Moderate Swing

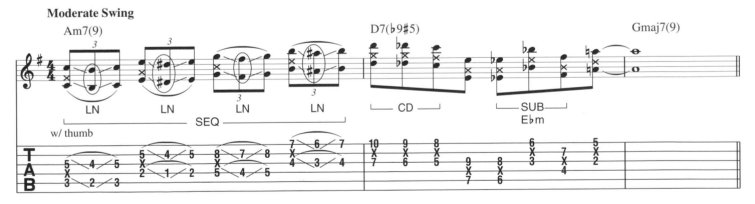

61 Basic Tonality: D Minor/G Dominant

Moderate Swing

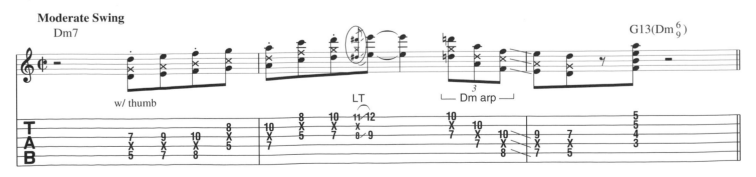

Modal Jazz

Modal jazz emerged in the late 1950s and early 1960s, and represented another alternative to bebop. Miles Davis is credited with developing this style on his *Kind of Blue* record of 1959, featuring an all-star lineup with saxophonists John Coltrane and Cannonball Adderley and pianist Bill Evans. Since then, tunes like 'So What," "Milestones,"and "Impressions" have become standard vehicles of modern jazz. Historically, modal jazz set the stage for jazz-rock fusion in the years to follow and influenced many rock players of the 1960s.

Modal jazz can be defined as improvisation based on scales and modes rather than running chord changes. The modal style is dependent on static or slower-moving harmonic rhythm. Jazz musicians playing modal tunes frequently depart from the strict use of one particular scale or tonality in a solo. When an alternate scale is obtained from a remote source melodically or harmonically, it is often called "outside" (outside of the tonal center). Skilled players of modal jazz generally approach their improvisations as melodic motion from "inside" to "outside" and back in a juxtaposition of diatonic versus atonal sounds. In the following set of licks, note the use of related and unrelated alternate scales and extended arpeggios, and the resulting consonant-dissonant effect. Among the most successful modal jazz players are guitarists Wes Montgomery, George Benson, and Pat Martino.

These licks were played with a new Gibson ES-175D with humbuckers and a 1965 Fender Twin-Reverb amp.

62 **Basic Tonality: B Minor (Dorian)**

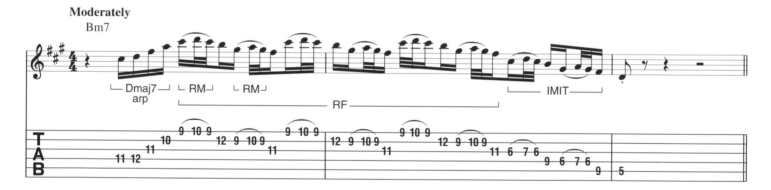

63 **Basic Tonality: D Minor**

28

64 Basic Tonality: A Minor

Moderately Fast Swing

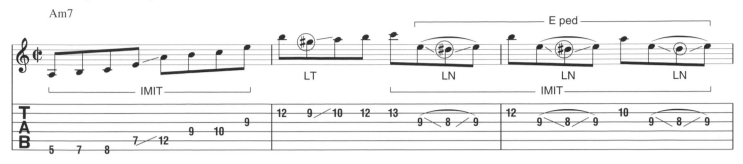

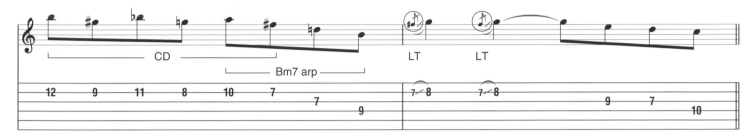

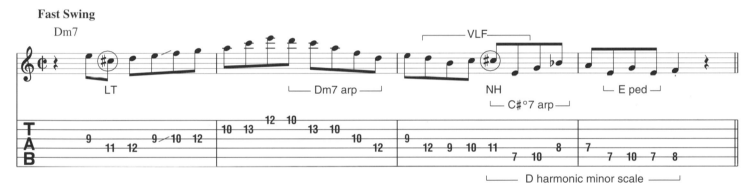

65 Basic Tonality: D Minor

Fast Swing

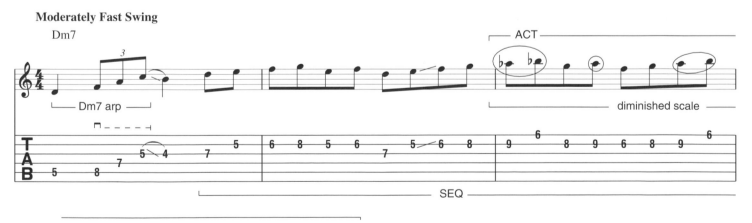

66 Basic Tonality: D Minor/G Dominant

Moderately Fast Swing

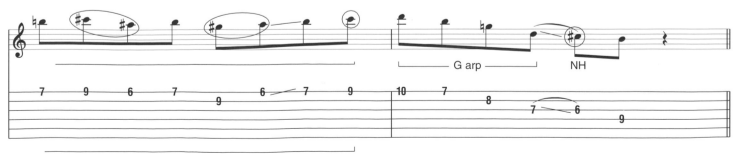

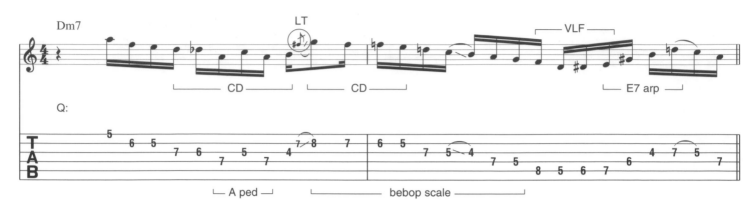

Moderately Fast

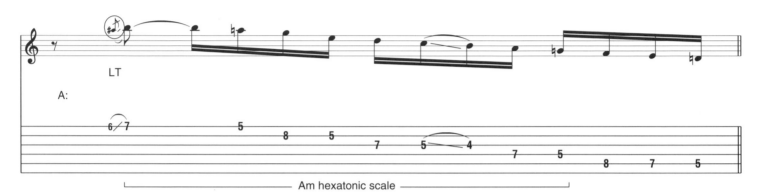

68 **Basic Tonality: D Minor**

Moderate Swing

69 Basic Tonality: D Minor

Moderately

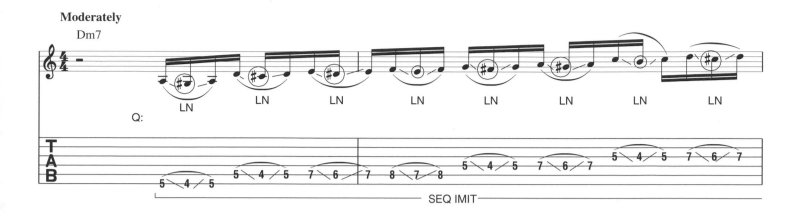

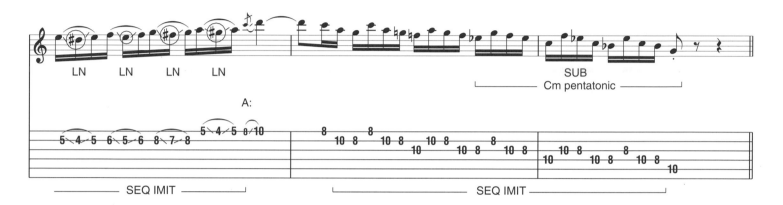

70 Basic Tonality: D Minor

Moderately

Soul Jazz

The blues has exerted a profound influence on jazz; in fact, the two are inextricably bound. The greatest jazz musicians have always displayed a formidable command of blues. In the early 1960s, a blues-based subgenre of jazz emerged that proved to the most popular of the period. An outgrowth of hard bop, it was dubbed *soul jazz* (also called "funky jazz") and flaunted an overt blues influence with an emphasis on gospel—evident in the "churchy" organ licks, strong melodies, and simplified, catchy rhythmic grooves. Soul jazz is epitomized by the organ-led groups of Jimmy Smith, Jack McDuff, Groove Holmes, and Don Patterson, who made extensive use of the organ-guitar-drums combination as their nucleus. A number of jazz guitarists gravitated to this style including Howard Roberts, Wes Montgomery, Kenny Burrell, Grant Green, Joe Pass, George Benson, and Pat Martino.

These licks were played on a Gibson ES-175/CC, an ES-175 with humbuckers, and a modified ES-150 (the "Black Guitar" previously owned by Howard Roberts) equipped with a P-90 pickup. For amplification, I again used a 1965 Fender Twin-Reverb.

71 Basic Tonality: G Dominant

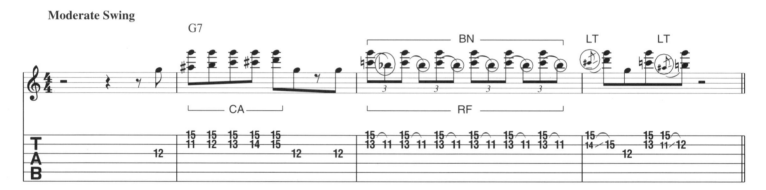

72 Basic Scale: G Blues

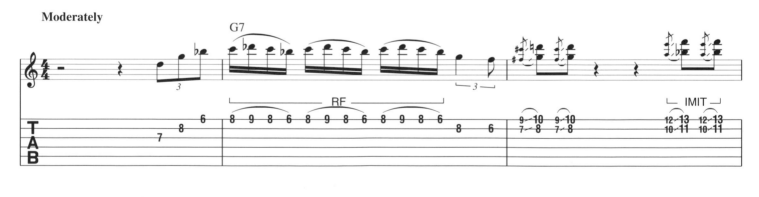

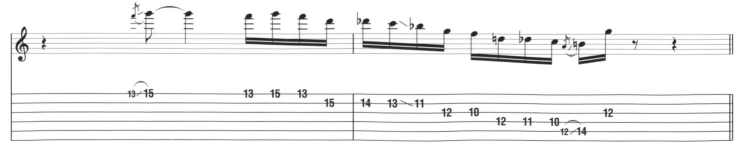

73 Basic Tonality: F Dominant

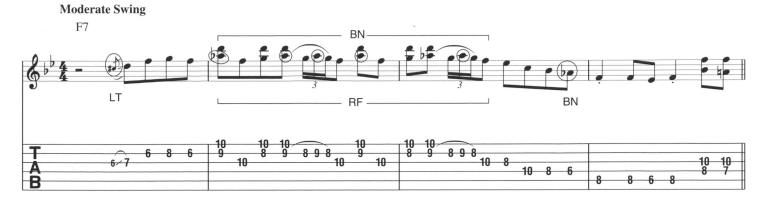

74 Basic Tonality: B♭ Dominant

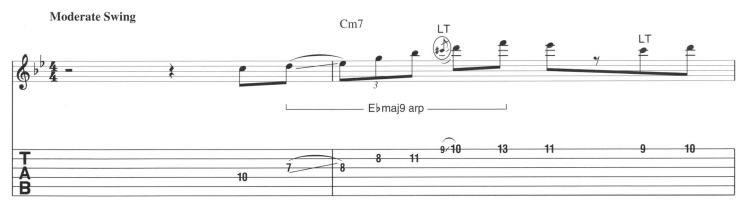

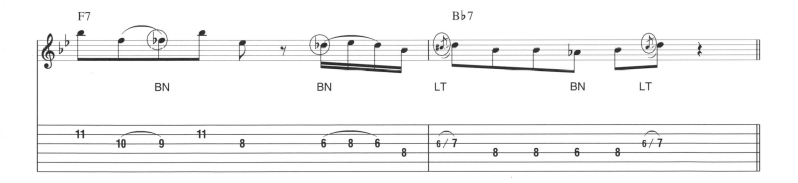

75 Basic Tonality: C Dominant

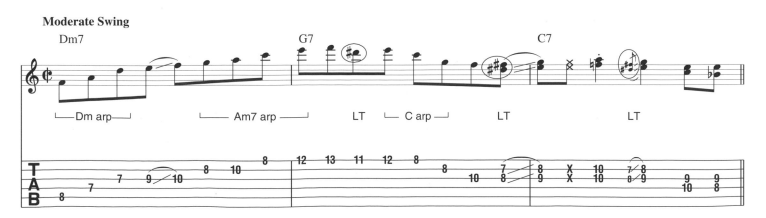

Postmodern Jazz

Postmodern jazz loosely refers to a general conglomeration of schools intent on modernizing the harmonic and melodic conventions of advanced bop, often blending it with twentieth-century dissonance and atonality. On the guitar, postmodern bop classicism is epitomized by the long winding lines of Pat Martino. The intervallic side of postmodern bop guitar is conveyed by Joe Diorio's abstract and angular melodic contours. Note the use of all twelve tones of the chromatic scale in Licks 81 and 82, typical of the genre.

The most controversial of the postmodern bop movements is the style known as *free jazz*. Free jazz, also called avante-garde and action jazz, was built on a foundation of 1950s bebop and is characterized by extreme chromaticism, use of very distant note-to-chord relationships (frequently to the point of atonality), extended "outside" playing often without traditional cadence formulas and resolutions, and the highest level of dissonance in jazz. The free jazz genre was formally born with the work of alto saxophonist Ornette Coleman on his 1958 recording *Something Else!* and reached fruition in the 1960s. In the 1990s, guitarist Pat Metheny applied many of Coleman's free jazz concepts in fashioning his own melodic approach and in improvising over standard tunes.

These licks were played on a new Gibson ES-175D and a Polytone Mini-Brute II amp.

76 **Basic Tonality: C Minor (Dorian)**

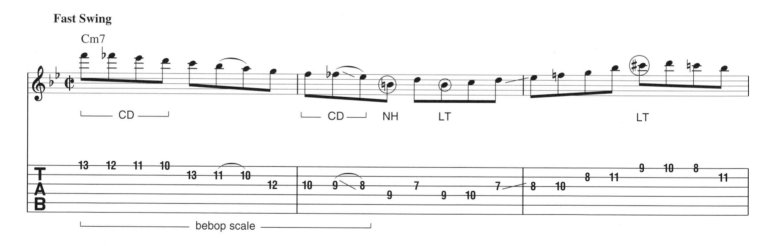

77 Basic Tonality: D Dominant

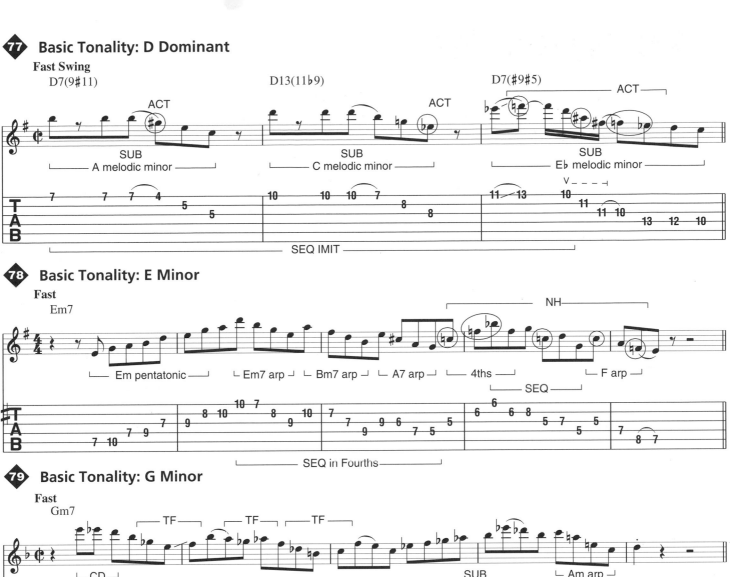

78 Basic Tonality: E Minor

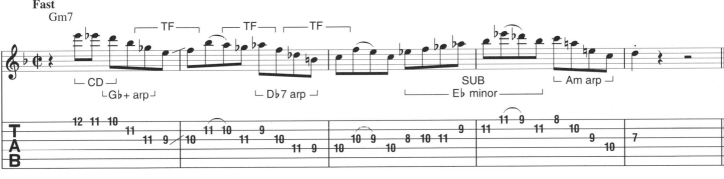

79 Basic Tonality: G Minor

80 Basic Tonality: E Dominant

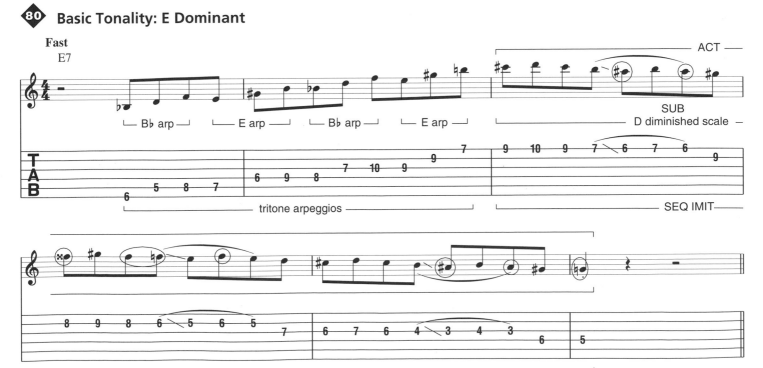

81 Basic Tonality: D Dominant

Fast

D7

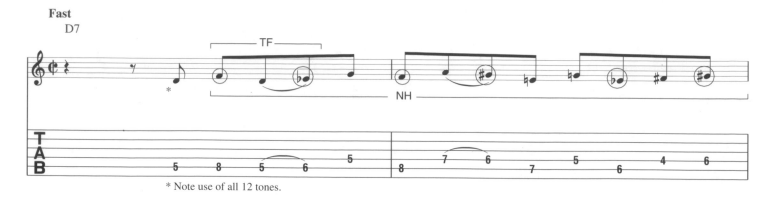

* Note use of all 12 tones.

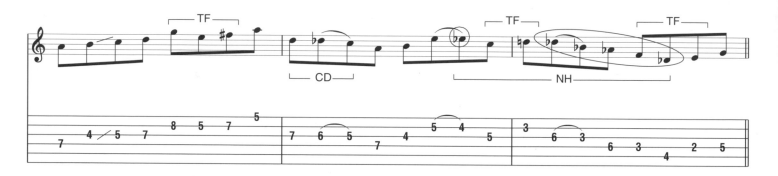

82 Basic Tonality: G Dominant

Fast

G7

* Note use of all 12 tones.

Jazz Chord Licks

The chord tradition in jazz guitar has had a venerable history. The earliest jazz guitarists were predominately chord stylists of the 1920s. Eddie Lang, Lonnie Johnson, Dick McDonough, and Carl Kress contributed some of the first salient examples. These players fostered the next generation of swing guitarists which included chord-melody master George Van Eps and rhythm guitar kingpin Freddie Green. In the post-swing bop era, a number of important chord-melody styles emerged via Johnny Smith, Barney Kessel, Jim Hall, Kenny Burrell, and Howard Roberts. Wes Montgomery upped the ante in the 1960s with his innovative block-chord approach. Joe Pass was the reigning chord-melody bop virtuoso of the last three decades notwithstanding significant offerings from Lenny Breau and George Benson.

This final batch of licks present a potpourri of jazz guitar chord styles spanning the past sixty-five years. They were played using a variety of Gibson archtop electrics and a Polytone Mini-Brute amp. The first two examples are typical of older swing rhythm styles and were played on a 1940 Gibson L-5 non-cutaway archtop acoustic with a DeArmond Rhythm Chief floating pickup.

83 **Basic Tonality: F Dominant**

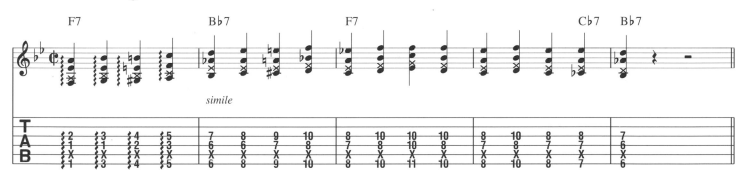

84 **Basic Tonality: G Major**

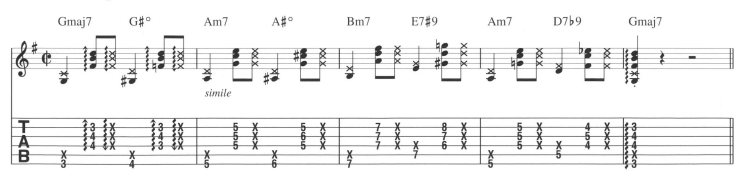

85 **Basic Tonality: C Major**

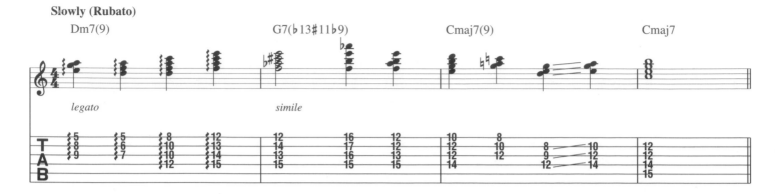

◀ ▶ Basic Tonality: C Major

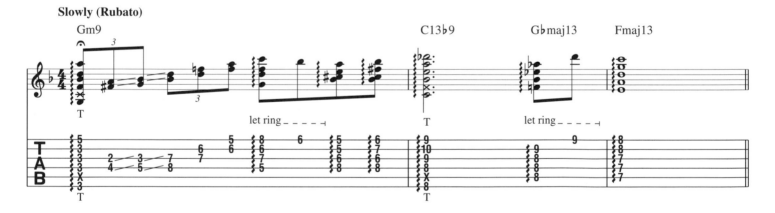

◀ ▶ Basic Tonality: F Major

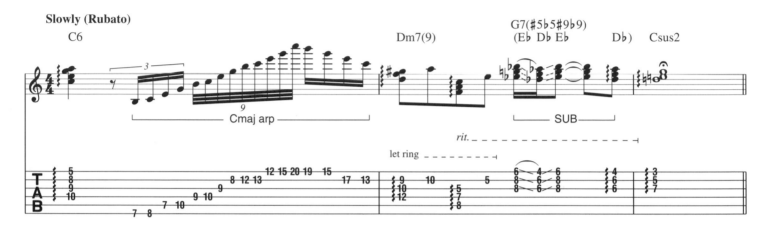

88 **Basic Tonality: B♭ Major**

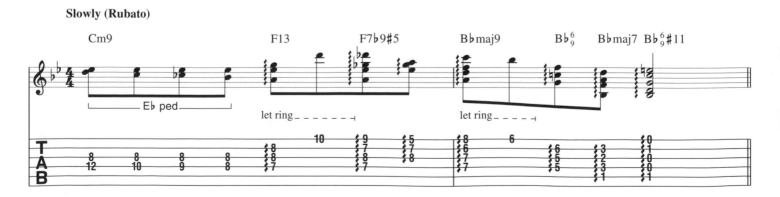

Basic Tonality: F Major

Moderately Fast Swing

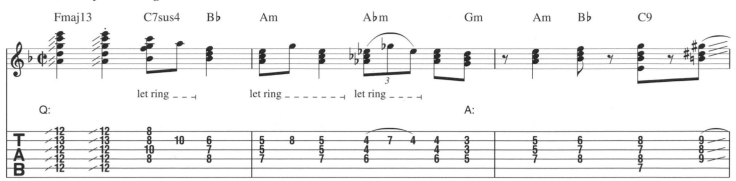

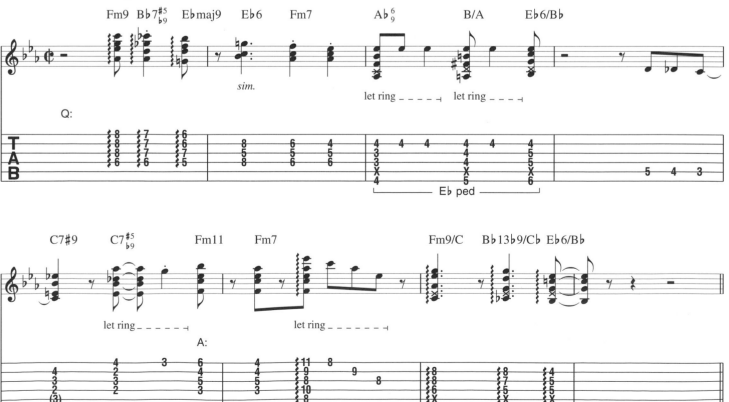

Basic Tonality: E♭ Major

Moderate Swing

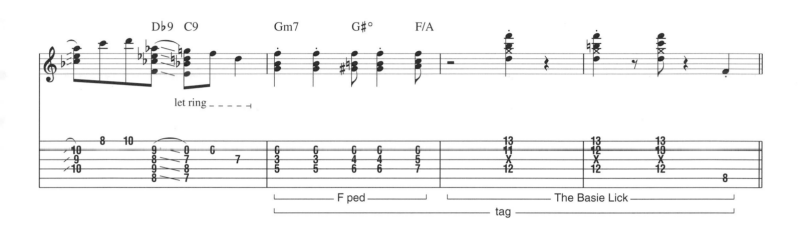

91 Basic Tonality: C Major/Dominant

Fast Swing

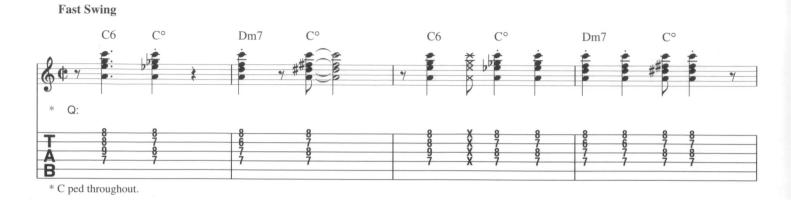

* C ped throughout.

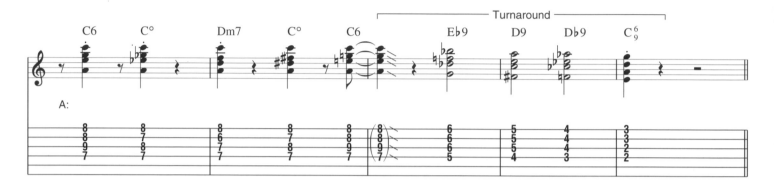

92 Basic Tonality: C Major

Moderate Swing

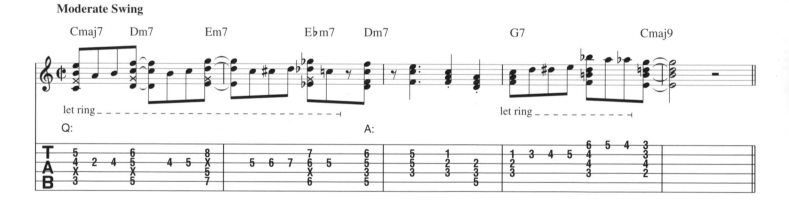

93 Basic Tonality: F Major

Moderate Swing

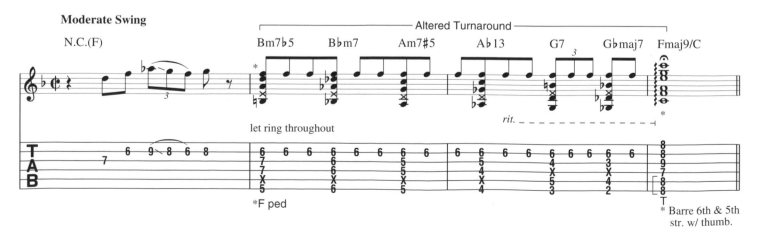

94 Basic Tonality: G Major

Moderate Swing

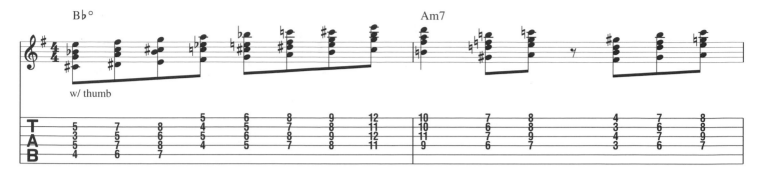

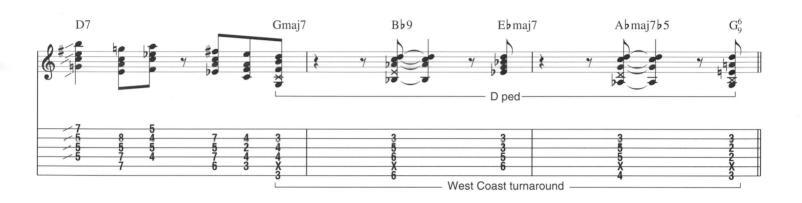

95 Basic Tonality: A Dominant

Moderate Swing

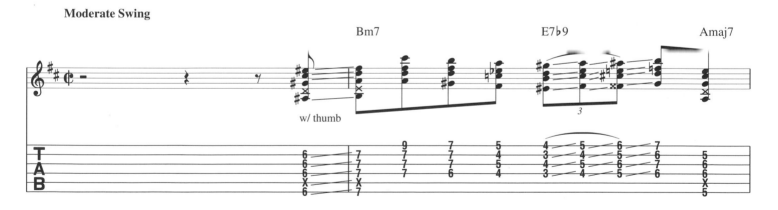

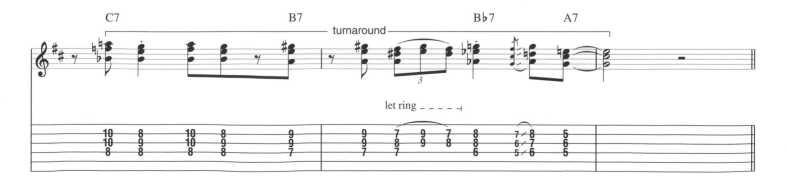

96 Basic Tonality: G Dominant

Moderately

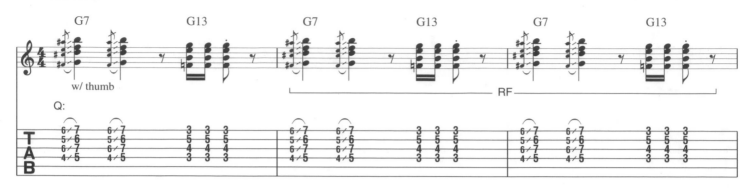

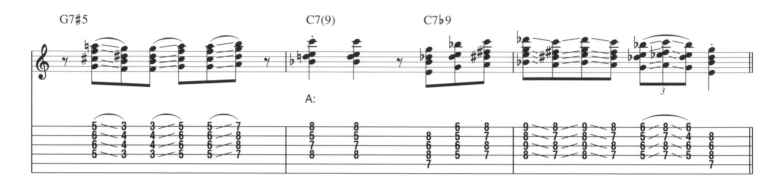

97 Basic Tonality: F Dominant

Moderate Swing

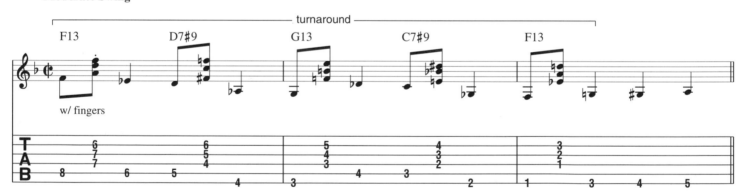

98 Basic Tonality: C Major

Slowly with Swing Feel (Rubato)

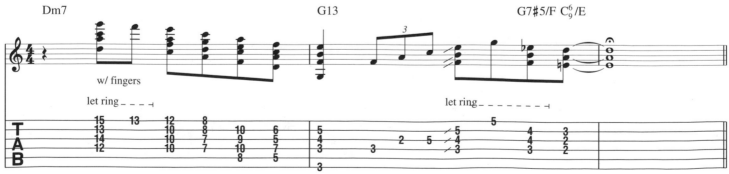

◆99 Basic Tonality: G Major ("Autumn Leaves" changes)

Moderate Swing

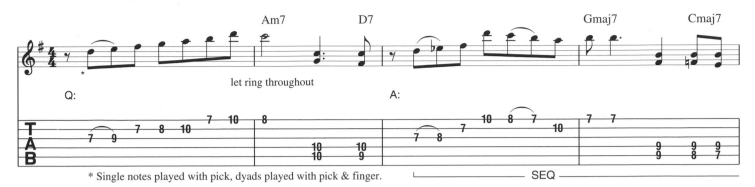

let ring throughout

* Single notes played with pick, dyads played with pick & finger.

SEQ

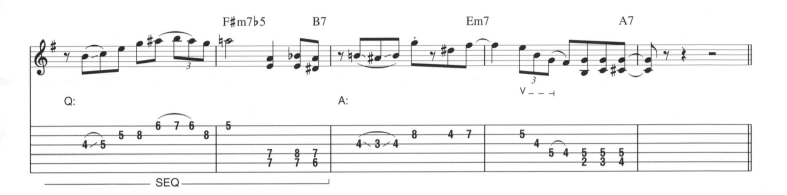

SEQ

* ◆99 [Lick 100] Basic Tonality: D Minor

Moderately with Swing Feel

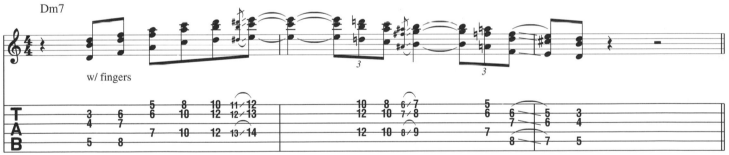

w/ fingers

* Lick 100 begins at 0:45 of Track 99.

* ◆99 [Lick 101] Basic Tonality: D Dominant

Moderately Slow (Rubato)

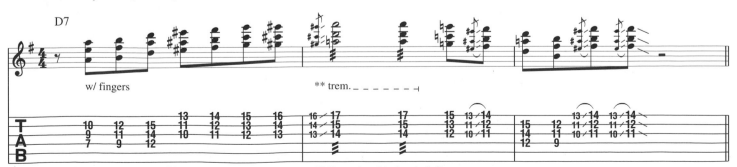

w/ fingers

** trem.

* Lick 101 begins at 1:04 of Track 99.

** Tremolo with thumb & fingers.

Suggested Recordings

Jazz music is a lifelong commitment. If you wish to explore the genre more thoroughly, here are some definitive recordings filled with must-know licks offered for your continuing study and appreciation.

Various: *Pioneers of the Jazz Guitar* (Yazoo)

Charlie Christian: *The Genius of the Electric Guitar* (Columbia)
Live Sessions at Minton's Playhouse 1941 (Jazz Anthology)

Django Reinhardt: *Django Reinhardt / Jazz Masters 38* (Verve)

George Van Eps: *Hand-Crafted Swing* (Concord Jazz)

Charlie Parker: *Yardbird Suite / The Ultimate Charlie Parker Collection* (Rhino)
Confirmation: The Best of the Verve Years (Verve)
Charlie Parker with Strings: The Master Takes (Verve)

Dizzy Gillespie: *Complete RCA Victor Recordings* (Bluebird)

Various: *Charlie Parker & Stars of Modern Jazz At Carnegie Hall* (Jass)

Barney Kessel: *Easy Like, Vol.1* (Original Jazz Classics)
The Poll Winners / Exploring the Scene (Contemporary)

Tal Farlow: *Tal Farlow / Jazz Masters 41* (Verve)
Chromatic Palette (Concord Jazz)

Jimmy Raney: *Stan Getz at Storyville, Vol. 1 & 2* (Roulette)
Visits Paris, Vol.1 (Vogue)

Johnny Smith: *Moonlight in Vermont* (Roulette)

Jim Hall: *Jazz Guitar* (Pacific Jazz)
Alone Together (Original Jazz Classics)

Herb Ellis: *Jazz at Concord* (Concord Jazz)

Kenny Burrell: *Blue Lights, Vol. 1-2* (Blue Note)
Kenny Burrell & John Coltrane (Original Jazz Classics)

Hank Garland: *Jazz Winds from a New Direction* (Sony Special Products)

Miles Davis: *Birth of the Cool* (Capitol)
Kind of Blue (Columbia)
Miles Smiles (Columbia)

John Coltrane: *Blue Train* (Blue Note)
Giant Steps (Atlantic)
Heavyweight Champion: The Complete Atlantic Recordings (Rhino/Atlantic)
A Love Supreme (Impulse!)

Howard Roberts:	*Dirty 'N' Funky* (EMI-Capitol Music)
	The Magic Band, Live at Donte's (V.S.O.P. #94)
Joe Pass:	*The Best of Joe Pass: Pacific Jazz Years* (Pacific Jazz)
	For Django (BGO Records)
	Virtuoso (Pablo)
Wes Montgomery:	*Fingerpickin'* (Pacific Jazz)
	Full House (Original Jazz Classics)
	The Complete Riverside Recordings (Riverside)
	Impressions: The Verve Jazz Sides (Verve)
Grant Green:	*Matador* (Blue Note)
	Idle Moments (Blue Note)
George Benson:	*This Is Jazz* (Columbia)
	Beyond the Blue Horizon (CTI-Columbia)
	Breezin' (Warner Bros.)
Pat Martino:	*East!* (Original Jazz Classics)
	Footprints (32 Jazz)
	Consciousness (Muse)
Emily Remler:	*Retrospective, Vol.1: Standards* (Concord Jazz)
Ornette Coleman:	*Something Else!* (Original Jazz Classics)
	Beauty Is a Rare Thing: The Complete Atlantic Recordings (Rhino/Atlantic)
Pat Metheny:	*Song X* (Geffen)
	Question and Answer (Geffen)
Henry Johnson:	*You're the One* (MCA)
Ron Eschete:	*Rain or Shine* (Concord Jazz)
Jimmy Bruno:	*Like That* (Concord Jazz)
Ron Affif:	*52nd Street* (Pablo)
Russell Malone:	*Russell Malone* (Columbia)
Mark Whitfield:	*True Blue* (Verve)

About the Author

Wolf Marshall is the pre-eminent guitar educator-performer of our time. The founder and original editor-in-chief of *GuitarOne* magazine, he is a highly respected and prolific author and columnist who has been an influential force in music education since the early 1980s. Wolf has worked closely with Hal Leonard Corporation for the past decade, authoring such highly acclaimed multimedia books as *The Guitar Style of Stevie Ray Vaughan, Stevie Ray Vaughan, Blues Guitar Classics, The Beatles Favorites, The Beatles Hits, The Rolling Stones, The Best of Carlos Santana, Guitar Instrumental Hits, Steve Vai: Alien Love Secrets, Eric Clapton Unplugged, Eric Johnson, The Guitars of Elvis, Aerosmith 1973-1979* and *Aerosmith 1979-1998, Acoustic Guitar of the '60s and '70s, Acoustic Guitar of the '80s and '90s, Mark Knopfler, The Best of Queen, The Best of Cream,* and many more. His eight-volume series *The Wolf Marshall Guitar Method* and *Power Studies* established new standards for modern guitar pedagogy in the early 1990s, as did his *Guitar Jammin'* authentic song books.

In *101 Must-Know Jazz Licks,* and its predecessor *101 Must-Know Blues Licks,* Wolf directs his encyclopedic knowledge of modern guitar music at a unique series designed to improve the vocabulary of all guitarists. The list of his credits is immense and can be found at his web site: *www.wolfmarshall.com.*

Guitar Notation Legend

Guitar music can be notated three different ways: on a *musical staff*, in *tablature*, and in *rhythm slashes*.

RHYTHM SLASHES are written above the staff. Strum chords in the rhythm indicated. Use the chord diagrams found at the top of the first page of the transcription for the appropriate chord voicings. Round noteheads indicate single notes.

THE MUSICAL STAFF shows pitches and rhythms and is divided by bar lines into measures. Pitches are named after the first seven letters of the alphabet.

TABLATURE graphically represents the guitar fingerboard. Each horizontal line represents a a string, and each number represents a fret.

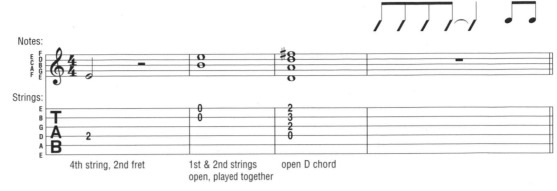

4th string, 2nd fret   1st & 2nd strings open, played together   open D chord

Definitions for Special Guitar Notation

HALF-STEP BEND: Strike the note and bend up 1/2 step.

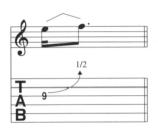

WHOLE-STEP BEND: Strike the note and bend up one step.

GRACE NOTE BEND: Strike the note and bend up as indicated. The first note does not take up any time.

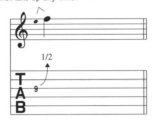

SLIGHT (MICROTONE) BEND: Strike the note and bend up 1/4 step.

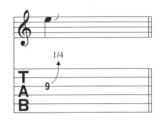

BEND AND RELEASE: Strike the note and bend up as indicated, then release back to the original note. Only the first note is struck.

PRE-BEND: Bend the note as indicated, then strike it.

PRE-BEND AND RELEASE: Bend the note as indicated. Strike it and release the bend back to the original note.

UNISON BEND: Strike the two notes simultaneously and bend the lower note up to the pitch of the higher.

VIBRATO: The string is vibrated by rapidly bending and releasing the note with the fretting hand.

WIDE VIBRATO: The pitch is varied to a greater degree by vibrating with the fretting hand.

HAMMER-ON: Strike the first (lower) note with one finger, then sound the higher note (on the same string) with another finger by fretting it without picking.

PULL-OFF: Place both fingers on the notes to be sounded. Strike the first note and without picking, pull the finger off to sound the second (lower) note.

LEGATO SLIDE: Strike the first note and then slide the same fret-hand finger up or down to the second note. The second note is not struck.

SHIFT SLIDE: Same as legato slide, except the second note is struck.

TRILL: Very rapidly alternate between the notes indicated by continuously hammering on and pulling off.

TAPPING: Hammer ("tap") the fret indicated with the pick-hand index or middle finger and pull off to the note fretted by the fret hand.

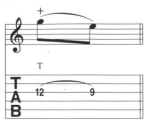

NATURAL HARMONIC: Strike the note while the fret-hand lightly touches the string directly over the fret indicated.

PINCH HARMONIC: The note is fretted normally and a harmonic is produced by adding the edge of the thumb or the tip of the index finger of the pick hand to the normal pick attack.

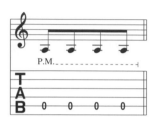

HARP HARMONIC: The note is fretted normally and a harmonic is produced by gently resting the pick hand's index finger directly above the indicated fret (in parentheses) while the pick hand's thumb or pick assists by plucking the appropriate string.

PICK SCRAPE: The edge of the pick is rubbed down (or up) the string, producing a scratchy sound.

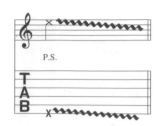

MUFFLED STRINGS: A percussive sound is produced by laying the fret hand across the string(s) without depressing, and striking them with the pick hand.

PALM MUTING: The note is partially muted by the pick hand lightly touching the string(s) just before the bridge.

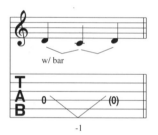

RAKE: Drag the pick across the strings indicated with a single motion.

TREMOLO PICKING: The note is picked as rapidly and continuously as possible.

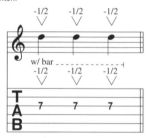

ARPEGGIATE: Play the notes of the chord indicated by quickly rolling them from bottom to top.

VIBRATO BAR DIVE AND RETURN: The pitch of the note or chord is dropped a specified number of steps (in rhythm) then returned to the original pitch.

VIBRATO BAR SCOOP: Depress the bar just before striking the note, then quickly release the bar.

VIBRATO BAR DIP: Strike the note and then immediately drop a specified number of steps, then release back to the original pitch.

Additional Musical Definitions

 (accent) • Accentuate note (play it louder)

 (accent) • Accentuate note with great intensity

 (staccato) • Play the note short

 • Downstroke

V • Upstroke

D.S. al Coda • Go back to the sign (𝄋), then play until the measure marked "***To Coda***," then skip to the section labelled "***Coda***."

D.S. al Fine • Go back to the beginning of the song and play until the measure marked "***Fine***" (end).

Rhy. Fig. • Label used to recall a recurring accompaniment pattern (usually chordal).

Riff • Label used to recall composed, melodic lines (usually single notes) which recur.

Fill • Label used to identify a brief melodic figure which is to be inserted into the arrangement.

Rhy. Fill • A chordal version of a Fill.

tacet • Instrument is silent (drops out).

 • Repeat measures between signs.

 • When a repeated section has different endings, play the first ending only the first time and the second ending only the second time.

NOTE: Tablature numbers in parentheses mean:
1. The note is being sustained over a system (note in standard notation is tied), or
2. The note is sustained, but a new articulation (such as a hammer-on, pull-off, slide or vibrato begins, or
3. The note is a barely audible "ghost" note (note in standard notation is also in parentheses).